WONDERFUL
WORLD OF
ANIMALS

This 1997 edition published by Brockhampton Press
20 Bloomsbury Street, London WC1B 3QA

Text by Beatrice MacLeod
Designed by Marco Nardi
Illustrated by Antonella Pastorelli

Created and produced by McRae Books Srl
Via dei Rustici, 5 – Florence, Italy

ISBN 1-86019-588-1

WONDERFUL WORLD OF ANIMALS

AMPHIBIANS

Beatrice MacLeod
Illustrated by Antonella Pastorelli

BROCKHAMPTON PRESS

WHAT IS AN AMPHIBIAN?

Amphibians vary enormously in size and shape. For example, some amphibians have long tails while others have none at all; some have four legs, some have two, and others have no legs. Unlike other vertebrates, which have hair, feathers or scales to protect their bodies, amphibians have bare skin. They are divided into three groups.

Amphibians in the **Urodela** group have tails. This group includes newts, salamanders and sirens.

Fire salamander

The second, and largest, group of amphibians is composed of frogs and toads. The group is called **Anura**, which means 'without tails'. Adult frogs and toads do not have tails.

Green toad

Caecilian

The third group is called **Gymnophiona** and is made up of caecilians. They have no legs and look like earthworms.

BORN IN THE WATER

The word 'amphibian' comes from two ancient Greek words – *amphi* ('both') and *bios* ('life'). A typical amphibian spends its youth (larval stages) in the water and its adult life on land.

1. Frogs, for example, lay their eggs in the water. The soft eggs are protected by a jelly-like coating.

2. After about a week, the embryos have developed heads and tails.

3. When the tadpoles hatch, they have external gills and can swim using their tails. They have no legs (they develop later).

4. After a few weeks (or months, or even, in some species, years), the tadpole is completely transformed. The adult frog has no gills or tail. It has lungs and breathes directly from the air.

North American leopard frog

Amphibians in the story of evolution
Life began in the water about 4500 million years ago. Over millions of years fish developed. Amphibians, the first animals able to breathe air and live on land, evolved from fish. In turn, amphibians gave rise to reptiles, birds and mammals.

LAND OR WATER?

Not all amphibians grow up in the water and spend their adult lives on land. Many species of salamander, for example, live and breed entirely on land. Some other amphibians spend all their lives in the water.

Salamanders that reproduce on land lay their eggs in damp places, such as in rotting tree trunks. The larval stage is passed within the egg and the salamander is formed before it hatches.

Salamander's egg

When the egg breaks a tiny **salamander** appears. It keeps its tail, while the gills disappear after a time.
In some species the gills remain in adulthood.

Young tiger salamander

Most **newts** spend spring and summer in the water. They lay their eggs in spring and then build up reserves of fat ready to spend the winter on land.

Red-spotted newt

FROGS AND TOADS

Most frogs and toads live in tropical and subtropical regions. A few species also live in other environments, including deserts, mountains, grasslands, woods and cities. They live on every continent except Antarctica.

Toads live in damp, dark places, often far from water. They are mainly active at night, or dusk and dawn, when they hunt for insects and small animals. Most species return to the water to breed.

Common toad

Surinam toad

The **Surinam toad** is a strange, tongueless toad. It has a flat body and a large triangular head. Surinam toads spend all their lives in the water. During reproduction, the male toad presses the fertilized eggs onto the female's back. A special protective skin grows around the eggs. After about 80 days the young hatch as fully-formed miniature toads.

Frog or toad?

Most frogs have smooth, muscus-covered skins, and long powerful back legs. They move by jumping and live in or near water. Almost all toads have squat bodies, short legs and dry, rough skins. Less active than frogs, toads usually move on land by walking.

Salamanders and Newts

Salamanders and newts live in cool temperate regions. Only one group of salamanders lives in the tropical zones of Central and South America. They inhabit a variety of habitats. Aquatic species live in rivers, lakes and swamps. Land-dwellers live under rocks and logs. Some species burrow into the soil.

The North American **many-ribbed salamander** is one of many species of lungless salamanders. They breathe through their skin and the lining of their mouths.

Many-ribbed salamander

Two-lined salamander

Aquatic **salamanders** and newts are good swimmers. They move on land using their short legs and sinuous body movements. When danger threatens they can move quickly.

In spring, all **newts** and many salamanders return to the river or pond where they were born to breed. They sometimes travel several miles. They have a good sense of direction.

Marbled newt

13

GETTING AROUND

Amphibians have more or less developed tails, legs and organs according to the environment in which they live. An olm's streamlined body and long tail are ideal for swimming, whereas the toad's well-developed hind legs are useful for swimming and essential for leaping.

The **olm**, a blind salamander, lives in underwater caves in southeastern Europe. It has bright red gills, a long pale body (up to 28 centimetres in length), and tiny limbs.

Olm

The **tree-toad** has sticky spots on its fingers which help it cling to and move over smooth or slippery surfaces. Its powerful back legs allow it make long leaps to escape from a predator and to surprise an insect or small animal.

European tree-toad

Cold-blooded animals
To maintain a constant body temperature, mammals and birds (warm-blooded animals) must eat regularly. Amphibians (called cold-blooded animals) are able to adapt their body temperature to the surrounding environment. They use less energy and need less food.

WATER IS LIFE

Amphibians have soft, unprotected skins. They live in moist places to avoid drying out. On land they stay under damp debris or near the water. Some species, like the garden toad, stay in burrows during the day and only come out at night when there is more moisture about.

Male crested newt

The **crested newt** of Europe and Asia grows up to 20 centimetres long. It has a rough warty skin. It gets its name from the crest which appears along the male's back and head during courtship. The male, slightly smaller than the female, does a very elaborate courtship dance.

Yellow fire-bellied toad

Fire-bellied toads have brightly coloured bellies. When danger threatens, they display their undersides to warn predators that their skin is poisonous. They live in ponds and feed on insects.

Caecilian

Caecilians live in tropical regions. They are burrowing animals. They use their heads to dig burrows and poke them into soil or mud in search of food. Caecilians vary greatly in size. Some of the smallest species are only about 8 centimetres long, while the larger ones measure nearly 1.5 metres.

FOOD

Amphibians eat other animals, including worms, spiders, termites and insects of all sorts. Some species will eat almost anything they can catch, even quite large fish, reptiles or mammals.

Japanese giant salamander

The **Japanese giant salamander** measures up to 1.5 metres in length. It lives in mountain streams where it feeds on almost any other animal it can find.

A frog's tongue is attached to the front of its mouth. Its long sticky tongue is a formidable hunting weapon.

The bull frog and the **South American horned frog** are among the fiercest amphibians. With their huge mouths horned frogs can swallow a whole mouse!

South American horned frog

19

Fancy Colours

Many amphibians are brightly coloured with vividly patterned or marked skins. The colours are produced by three skin pigments (brown, yellow and white). Some amphibians can change colour. Amphibians use skin colour for camouflage, to hunt without being seen, to warn predators that they are poisonous and to recognize others of the same species.

Tiny **Darwin's frog** conceals itself from predators by way of its dark green skin which blends in with surrounding leaves. The male frog keeps its eggs and young in its vocal pouch until they can look after themselves.

Darwin's frog

Arrow-poison frog

"Watch out. I'm poisonous!" South American **arrow-poison frogs** use their bright colours to warn predators that their skin is poisonous. The poison is produced by glands in the skin, and can kill predators in record time.

Many animals keep safe by pretending to be more dangerous than they really are. Some harmless amphibians look like poisonous species, thus scaring off predators such as birds, snakes or other amphibians. Salamanders and newts have special glands on their skins which give off repulsive odours.

Salamander

METAMORPHOSIS

Metamorphosis is the term used to describe the transformations amphibians undergo when they pass from the aquatic larval stage to adulthood. The process can last from just a few days to several years, depending on the species. Some amphibians keep some juvenile features even as adults.

Axolotl

The **axolotl** is a large salamander. Most individuals in the species never loose their larval features (such as external gills).

The **rain frog** lives in the hot tropical rain forests of Central and South America. Baby frogs develop inside a large, clear egg without ever becoming tadpoles or undergoing metamorphosis.

Amphibian records

The tiny, 12 millimetres Cuban frog is the smallest amphibian known. The Chinese giant salamander is the largest species of amphibian alive today. The average adult weighs about 25 kilograms and is over 1 metre long.

Above: *South American rain froglet developing inside an egg*

PARENTAL CARE

Most amphibians lay eggs. Some females lay them in the water and leave them to hatch and take care of themselves as they grow. Other amphibian parents dedicate a lot of time to caring for their offspring.

After the female **midwife frog** lays her eggs (strings of about 40-50 eggs), the male attaches them to his hind legs where he keeps them safe and moist for about 3 weeks until they hatch as tadpoles.

Male midwife toad

A female pygmy marsupial frog in a bromeliad. Note the pouch with eggs on her back.

The female **pygmy marsupial frog** keeps her eggs in a pouch on her back until they hatch. She then deposits each tadpole in a water-filled bromeliad. Each week she returns to the bromeliad and lays a small clutch of unfertilized eggs on which her tadpole feeds until it turns into a frog.

Frogs' and toads' eggs

Depending on the species, frogs and toads lay anywhere between five and several thousand eggs in the water, on land, in trees or on the male or female's body. Laid together in blobs or long strings, the eggs are wrapped in a jelly-like substance or a protective foam.

FROGS' CHORUS

Male frogs and toads make a variety of calls, each with its own special meaning. They call to attract females, discourage rivals and to recognize others of the same species. Sometimes thousands of frogs call together, making a frogs' chorus.

Rush frog

This male **rush frog** has puffed its vocal pouch full of air ready to call for a female. As it breathes out the air will vibrate its vocal cords, producing the call.

When the male **tungara frog** puffs out its vocal pouch to call for a mate, it makes itself an easy target for predators. For this reason male tungara frogs stay together in groups when calling to confuse predators and in the hope that a neighbouring frog will be caught.

Types of call

Each species of frog or toad has its own special call. These range from croaks and clicks, to buzzing or humming sounds, to shrill whistles and trills. The length of the call can last from just a few milliseconds to several minutes.

INDEX